Jason's Quest
for the
Golden Fleece

By Anne Adeney

Illustrated by Graham Philpot

W

FRANKLIN WATTS

LONDON•SYDNEY

First published in 2009 by
Franklin Watts
338 Euston Road
London
NW1 3BH

Franklin Watts Australia
Level 17/207 Kent Street
Sydney
NSW 2000

Text © Anne Adeney 2009
Illustrations © Graham Philpot 2009

A CIP catalogue record for this book is available
from the British Library.

ISBN 978 0 7496 8587 4 (hbk)
ISBN 978 0 7496 8591 1 (pbk)

Series Editor: Melanie Palmer
Series Advisor: Dr Barrie Wade
Series Designer: Peter Scoulding

Printed in China

Franklin Watts is a division of
Hachette Children's Books,
an Hachette UK company
www.hachettelivre.co.uk

Long ago, Jason's wicked uncle,
Pelias, stole Jason's kingdom.
He sent Jason to an island far away.

3

Now Jason wanted it back.

He went to the royal palace.

"Give me my kingdom, Uncle!"

he demanded.

"First, prove you deserve it. Bring me the Golden Fleece," replied Pelias, grinning. "You'll have to ask old King Phineus where it is."

Jason built a special ship for the quest, called the "Argo".

He called his crew of fifty mighty heroes the "Argonauts".

They sailed to the island where old King Phineus lived. Harpies, horrible birds with human heads, were attacking the King.

Jason's crew shot their arrows at the Harpies and drove them away.

King Phineus was so grateful he told Jason where to find the Golden Fleece: "King Aites has it on the island of Colchis.

But beware of the Crashing Rocks," Phineus added. Jason smiled. He wasn't afraid of rocks!

But the rocks were huge!
They crashed together and
crushed everything between them.

Jason watched and had an idea. When the rocks opened he sent out a dove.

The rocks crashed ... but the dove
was through!

"GO!" Jason cried. The crew
rowed as fast as they could.
Then the rocks crashed again ...

... but the boat was through!

Jason sailed safely on to Colchis.
"I've come to take the Golden
Fleece," he told King Aites.

"First, tame my bulls, plough my field and sow these special seeds. Then I will give you the Fleece," said King Aites.

But the seeds were really dragon's teeth. Instead of plants, angry warriors sprang from the ground.

The warriors were made of bones. They didn't die, no matter how many times Jason used his sword.

So Jason threw a rock at one warrior.
"Who hit me?" yelled the warrior,
hitting another.

A fight began and soon all the warriors were dead and gone.

Jason went back to see King Aites.
"I'll never give you the Fleece!"
roared the King, angrily.

But the King's daughter, Medea,
had fallen in love with Jason.
"I'll take you to the Fleece," she said.

She led Jason to a dragon's lair.
By the dragon was a tree and
something gold and shiny.

The dragon breathed a ring of fire.
But Medea knew magic. She
charmed the dragon to sleep.

Jason leapt across the fire
and grabbed the Golden Fleece.
The Argonauts all cheered.

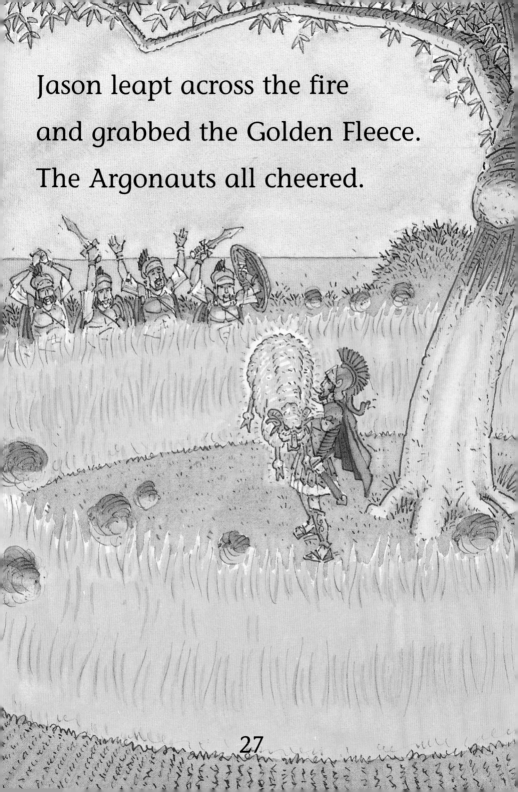

Medea joined Jason's ship and they sailed back to find Pelias.

Pelias was shocked to see Jason return. He ran away in fear, leaving Jason as the new King.

Puzzle 1

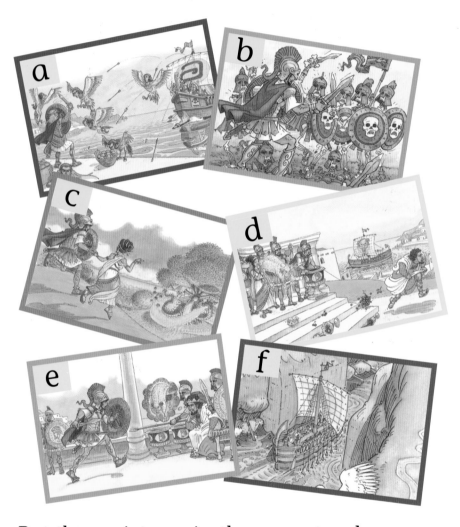

Put these pictures in the correct order.

Which event do you think is most important?

Now try writing the story in your own words!

30

Puzzle 2

Choose the correct speech bubbles for each character. Can you think of any others? Turn over to find the answers.

Answers

Puzzle 1

The correct order is

1e, 2a, 3f, 4b, 5c, 6d

Puzzle 2

Jason: 4, 6

Pelias: 1, 5

Medea: 2, 3

Look out for more Hopscotch Myths:

Icarus, the Boy Who Flew
ISBN 978 0 7496 7992 7*
ISBN 978 0 7496 8000 8

Perseus and the
Snake Monster
ISBN 978 0 7496 7993 4*
ISBN 978 0 7496 8001 5

Odysseus and the
Wooden Horse
ISBN 978 0 7496 7994 1*
ISBN 978 0 7496 8002 2

Persephone and the
Pomegranate Seeds
ISBN 978 0 7496 7995 8*
ISBN 978 0 7496 8003 9

Romulus and Remus
ISBN 978 0 7496 7996 5*
ISBN 978 0 7496 8004 6

Thor's Hammer
ISBN 978 0 7496 7997 2*
ISBN 978 0 7496 8005 3

Gelert the Brave
ISBN 978 0 7496 7999 6*
ISBN 978 0 7496 8007 7

No Dinner for Anansi
ISBN 978 0 7496 8006 0

King Midas's Golden Touch
ISBN 978 0 7496 8585 0*
ISBN 978 0 7496 8589 8

Theseus and the
Minotaur
ISBN 978 0 7496 8586 7*
ISBN 978 0 7496 8590 4

Jason's Quest for the
Golden Fleece
ISBN 978 0 7496 8587 4*
ISBN 978 0 7496 8591 1

Heracles and the
Terrible Tasks
ISBN 978 0 7496 8588 1*
ISBN 978 0 7496 8592 8

For more Hopscotch books go to: www.franklinwatts.co.uk

* hardback

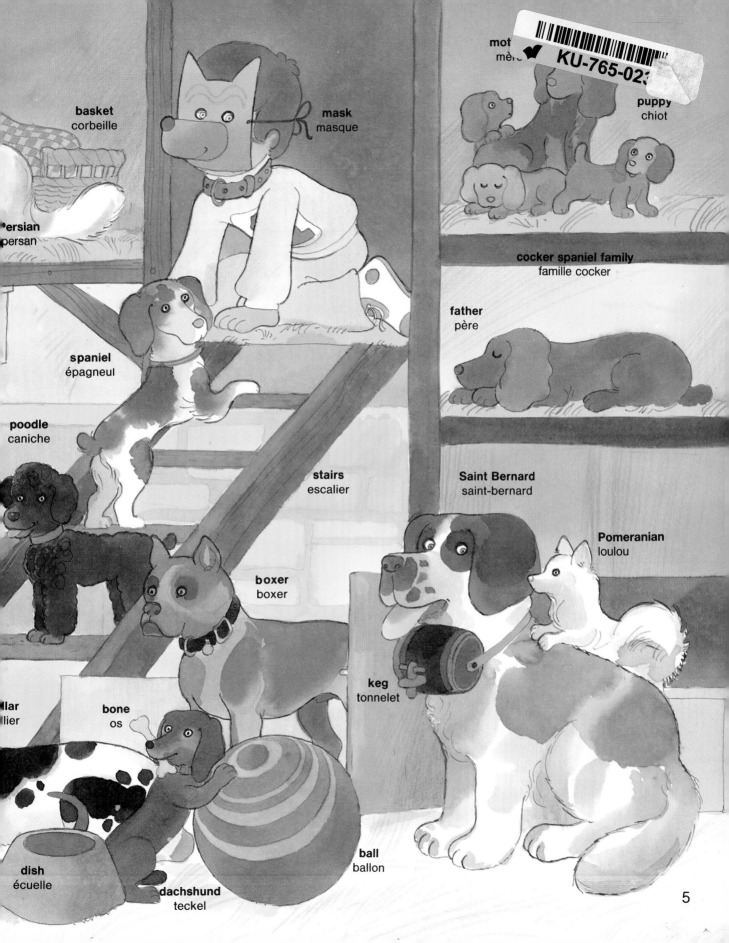

basket
corbeille

mask
masque

mot
mère

puppy
chiot

Persian
persan

cocker spaniel family
famille cocker

spaniel
épagneul

father
père

poodle
caniche

stairs
escalier

Saint Bernard
saint-bernard

Pomeranian
loulou

boxer
boxer

keg
tonnelet

lar
llier

bone
os

dish
écuelle

dachshund
teckel

ball
ballon

5

donkey
âne

bull
taureau

sheep
mouton

sow
truie

ewe
brebis

ram
bélier

rabbit
lapin

dog
chien

donkey foal
ânon

cow
vache

mule
mulet

From Donkey to Billy Goat

Our friends the Rascals have made up a matching game with the farm animals. But haven't they made a mistake in cutting the cards?

Jack

...ins a kilogram every month.

Ashley

is the most sentimental of all.

Paul

dreams only of setting sail.

Jason

loves artistic activities.

LEARN-A-WORD BOOKS
IN ENGLISH AND FRENCH

Animal Fun

227 Words in English and French

Text by Alain Grée
Illustrations by Luis Camps

AWARD PUBLICATIONS LTD – LONDON

ISBN 0-86163-375-X

Illustrations copyright © 1979 by Casterman. English
translation copyright © 1989 by Award Publications Limited.
...ch under the title *Les Farfeluches*
...les animaux.

...cations Limited, Spring House,
... Town, London NW5 3BH
...ts reserved.
Printed in Belgium

Like Cats and Dogs

When you like animals, it is fun to go and see the dogs and cats at the local pet shop. Hey, a newcomer has slipped in among the residents. Who could it be?

tabby kitten
chaton tigré

Siamese
siamois

comb
peigne

brush
brosse

PET SHOP
CHENIL

pet food
pâtée

muzzle
muselière

Alsatian
berger allemand

Afghan
lévrier afghan

lead
laisse

collie
colley

basset hound
basset

fox terrier
fox

4

horse
cheval

steer
boeuf

mare
jument

foal
poulain

nanny goat
chèvre

calf
veau

kid
chevreau

billy goat
bouc

7

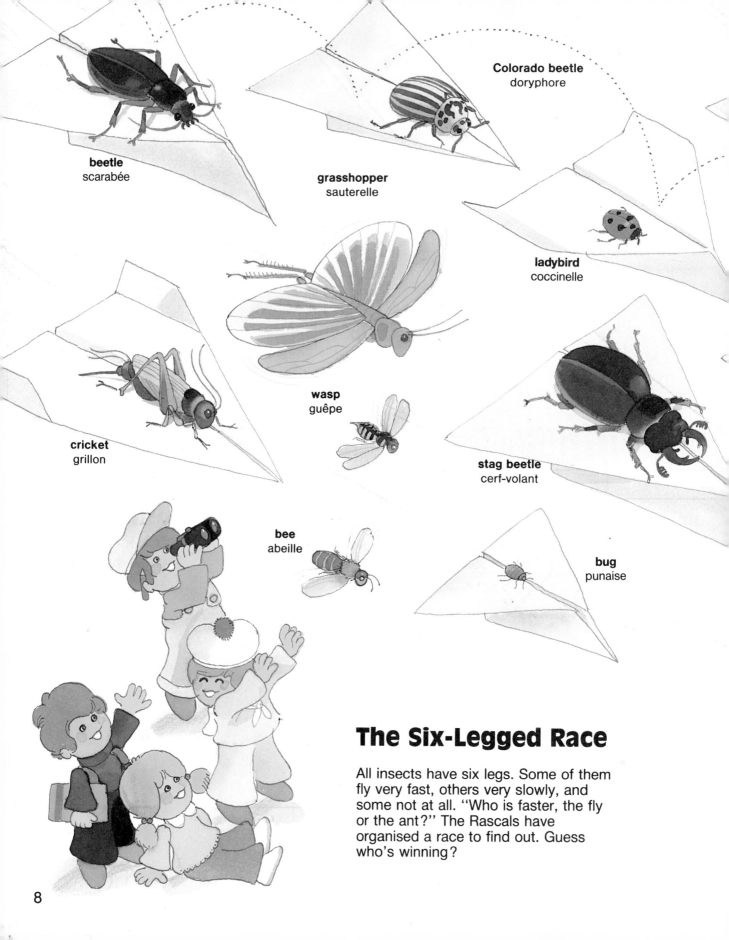

beetle
scarabée

Colorado beetle
doryphore

grasshopper
sauterelle

ladybird
coccinelle

cricket
grillon

wasp
guêpe

stag beetle
cerf-volant

bee
abeille

bug
punaise

The Six-Legged Race

All insects have six legs. Some of them fly very fast, others very slowly, and some not at all. "Who is faster, the fly or the ant?" The Rascals have organised a race to find out. Guess who's winning?

8

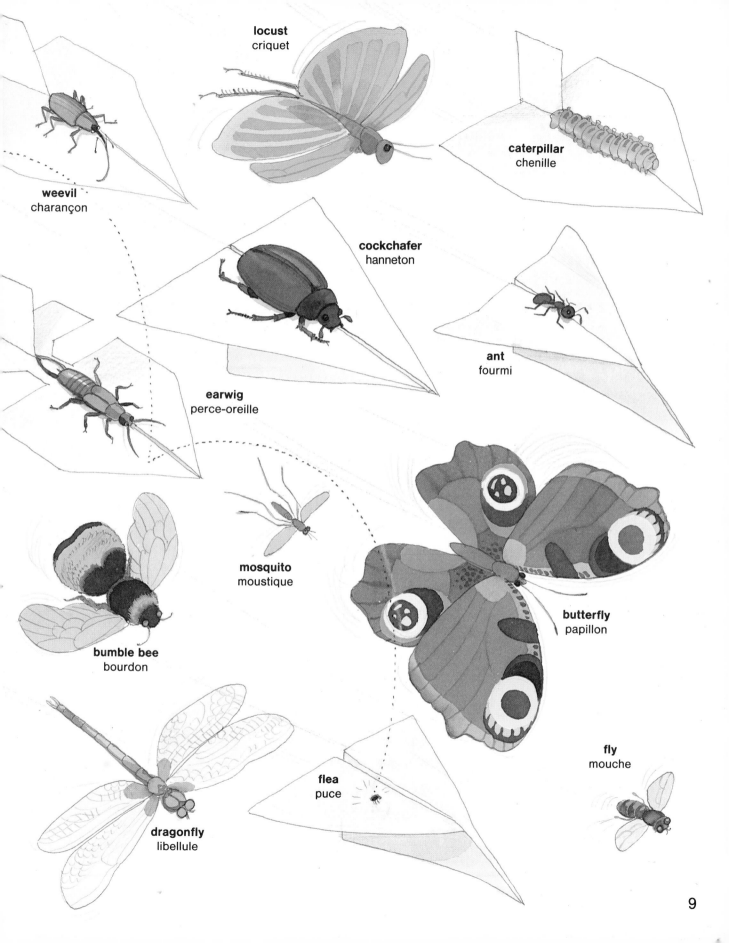

locust
criquet

caterpillar
chenille

weevil
charançon

cockchafer
hanneton

ant
fourmi

earwig
perce-oreille

mosquito
moustique

butterfly
papillon

bumble bee
bourdon

fly
mouche

dragonfly
libellule

flea
puce

9

wheel
roue

cap
casquette

otter
loutre

rasp
râpe

spider
araignée

jerboa
gerboise

stoat
hermine

pump
pompe

inner tube
chambre à air

shrew
musaraigne

viper
vipère

patches
pièces

snails
escargots

frog
grenouille

tortoise
tortue

10

pedal
pédale

A Ride in the Country...

Junior was riding along on his bicycle when, all of a sudden, a hedgehog appeared in front of him. "Right of way!" yelled Junior. But it was too late! The collision was inevitable. You can see the results.

light
phare

spanner
clé

mole
taupe

toad
crapaud

saddle
selle

glue
colle

handlebars
guidon

vole
campagnol

lizard
lézard

tyre
pneu

snake
couleuvre

weasel
belette

worm
orvet

field mouse
mulot

hedgehog
hérisson

slug
limace

hamster
hamster

11

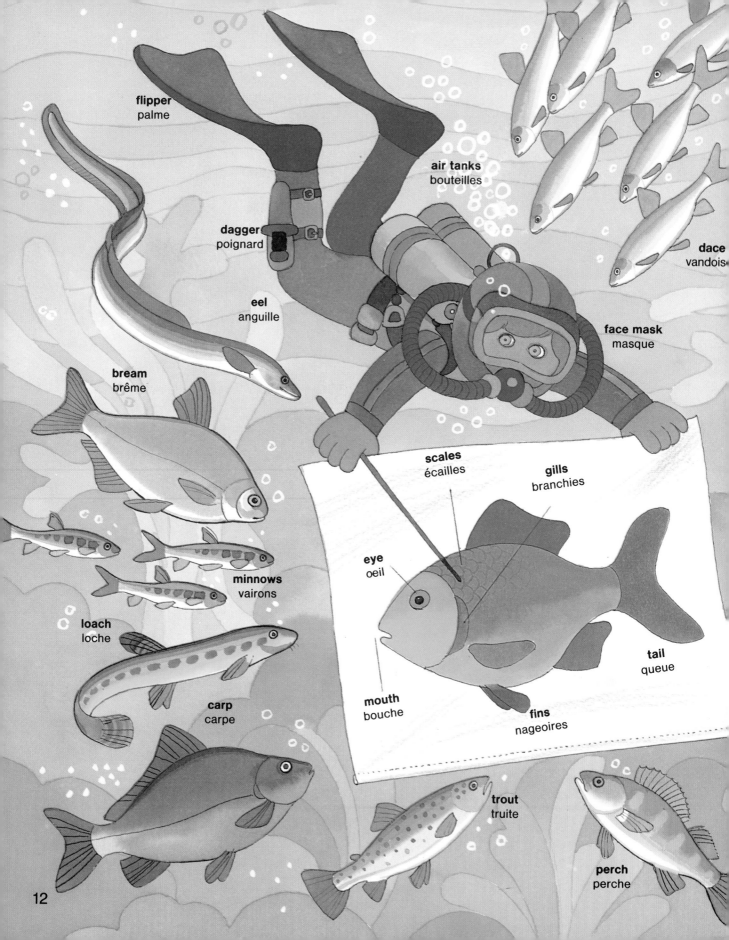

flipper
palme

air tanks
bouteilles

dace
vandois

dagger
poignard

eel
anguille

face mask
masque

bream
brême

scales
écailles

gills
branchies

eye
oeil

minnows
vairons

loach
loche

tail
queue

carp
carpe

mouth
bouche

fins
nageoires

trout
truite

perch
perche

12

roach
gardons

snorkel
tuba

catfish
barbeaux

camera
caméra

belt
ceinture

chub
chabots

wet suit
combinaison

salmon
saumon

tench
tanche

gudgeon
goujons

sturgeon
esturgeon

bleak
ablettes

Say It with Bubbles

On Sunday, the Rascals decided to play school with the fish in the river. First lesson: the parts of the body. Where are the scales? If you know the answer, raise your fin!

pike
brochet

13

Our Feathered Friends

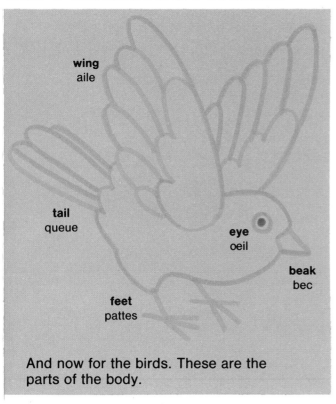

wing
aile

tail
queue

eye
oeil

beak
bec

feet
pattes

And now for the birds. These are the parts of the body.

woodpecker
pivert

raven
corbeau

kingfisher
martin-pêcheur

gull
mouette

Hey, someone has lost a feather. And here's another!

magpie
pie

owl
chouette

pigeon
pigeon

Mrs. Magpie shakes her head: "It's not mine. Look next door."

partridge
perdrix

parrot
perroquet

chaffinch
pinson

Not here either. No one has lost anything. Unless of course . . . it's . . .

14

eagle
aigle

parakeet
perruche

robin
rouge gorge

Here's yet another one. Someone is leaving his things all over the place this morning.

swallow
hirondelle

nightingale
rossignol

blackbird
merle

Whose green feather is this? No one answers. Is it yours, nightingale?

spear
lance

peace pipe
calumet

feathers
plumes

necklace
collier

bow
arc

moccasin
mocassin

hatchet
hache

arrows
flèches

. . a joke by the Rascal tribe!

15

A Special Report

The Rascals are making a special report for the school paper from the farmyard. "Ladies and gentlemen, would you mind saying a few words for our readers?"

cock pheasant
faisan

young pheasant
faisandeau

drake
canard

duckling
caneton

male pigeon
pigeon

duck
cane

female pigeon
pigeonne

As long as there's water so that we can swim, we are the happiest of all the animals in the farmyard. Who are we?

If you have an urgent message to send to school, you can count on me. I'm faster than the mail. What is my name?

turkey-hen
dinde

turkey-cock
dindon

I don't dance in nightclubs, but with my feathers, I would certainly be the star of the show. After the peacock, of course. Do you recognise me?

17

Rescue in the Forest

"Fire, fire! The forest is burning." The frightened animals run in every direction to get away from the flames. Luckily the Rascals have quickly built a raft. Everyone will be rescued just in time!

roe deer
chevreuil

polecat
putois

crate
caisse

squirrel
ecureuil

pole
perche

hind
biche

fox
renard

fallow deer
daim

net
épuisette

badger
blaireau

wolf
loup

smoke
fumée

red deer
cerf

wild boar
sanglier

dormouse
loir

hare
lièvre

plank
planche

racoon
raton-laveur

beaver
castor

pine marten
martre

stone marten
fouine

mouse
souris

barrel
tonneau

19

The Match-Up Game

The purpose of this game is to match up pairs (male and female) of animals. It is played by a group, with one die. The order of players is chosen at random, and the first player throws the die to designate the column (from 1 to 6). He or she then throws the die a second time and counts the circles, starting from the top. NOTE: If the number on the second roll is over 4, continue counting from bottom to top. EXAMPLE: first throw = 3 (3rd. column); second throw = 5, count: wild sow, boar, ewe, drake, and back up to ewe. Then the player has to find the animal that is the mate of the ewe. In our example the answer would be ''ram.'' If the player answers right the first time, he or she gets a point. Then it's the next player's turn.

ALSO: Earning 6 points allows the player to go again. The first player to reach 10 points wins. (The answers are at the back of the book).

20

1

horse
cheval

wild boar
sanglier

nanny goat
chèvre

cow
vache

2

gander
jars

bull
taureau

cockerel
coq

she wolf
louve

wild sow
laie

billy goat
bouc

wolf
loup

ram
bélier

boar
verrat

doe hare
hase

goose
oie

hare
lièvre

ewe
brebis

stag
cerf

mare
jument

duck
cane

drake
canard

hen
poule

hind
biche

sow
truie

21

Justine

is already a perfect homemaker.

Patrick

fights imaginary bandits.

Rudy

is only happy with a hammer in his hand.

Junior

is thirty-four kilos of muscle.

Max

hopes to be a pilot someday.

Peter

is more absent-minded than clumsy.